Who Was
Mark Twain?

SAMUEL LANGHORNE CLEMENS

Who Was
Mark Twain?

By April Jones Prince

Illustrated by John O'Brien

Grosset & Dunlap • New York

For David—the first writer in our family—
who always knows the difference between the
almost-right word and the right word—A.J.P.

To Tess—J.O.

Text copyright © 2004 by April Jones Prince. Illustrations copyright © 2004 by John
O'Brien. All rights reserved. Published by Grosset & Dunlap, a division of Penguin Young
Readers Group, 345 Hudson Street, New York, New York 10014. GROSSET & DUNLAP
is a trademark of Penguin Group (USA) Inc. Printed in the U.S.A.

Library of Congress Cataloging-in-Publication Data

Prince, April Jones.
  Who was Mark Twain? / by April Jones Prince ; illustrated by John O'Brien.
    v. cm.
Contents: Who was Mark Twain? — In with the comet — Life on the Mississippi —
Roughing it — The celebrated jumping frog — The Gilded Age — Tom and Huck —
Following the Equator — Waiting for the comet.
  ISBN 0-448-43537-3 (hardcover) — ISBN 0-448-43319-2 (pbk.)
  1. Twain, Mark, 1835–1910—Juvenile literature. 2. Authors, American—19th century—
Biography—Juvenile literature. [1. Twain, Mark, 1835–1910. 2. Authors, American.] I.
O'Brien, John, 1953– ill. II.
Title.
  PS1331.P7 2004
  818'.409—dc22
                                    2003021265

ISBN 0-448-43319-2 (pbk)   10 9 8 7 6 5 4 3 2 1
ISBN 0-448-43537-3 (GB)   10 9 8 7 6 5 4 3 2 1

Contents

Who Was
Mark Twain?

"When I was younger I could remember anything, whether it had happened or not."

—Mark Twain

If you can't quite place the name Mark Twain, think of *The Adventures of Tom Sawyer* and *The Adventures of Huckleberry Finn*: They're Mark Twain's most famous books.

Mark Twain was America's greatest storyteller. He was so good at making up stories that he even made up his name. (He was born Samuel Langhorne Clemens.) His best stories came from his own boyhood adventures in the Mississippi River town of Hannibal, Missouri.

Mark Twain had an exciting life—he was a steamboat pilot, a gold miner, a newspaper reporter. He trav-eled all around the world giving lectures—which were really more like one-man shows—about his writing and experiences. Mark Twain became the most famous and successful author of his day. Many of his stories are funny, but often the humor touches serious issues, including racism, greed, and injustice. America changed a great deal during Mark Twain's life. He challenged Americans to look at who they were and where they were going.

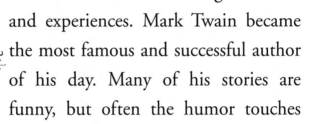

Chapter 1
In with the Comet

"There comes a time in every rightly constructed boy's life when he has a raging desire to go somewhere and dig for treasure."

—Mark Twain

Samuel Langhorne Clemens, the man who became famous as Mark Twain, was born in a two-room house in Florida, Missouri. The date was November 30, 1835.

HALLEY'S COMET

A COMET IS A BALL OF DUST, GASES, SNOW, AND ICE THAT TRAVELS AROUND THE SOLAR SYSTEM. WE CAN SEE COMETS EVERY ONCE IN A WHILE, WHEN THEY TRAVEL CLOSE TO THE SUN. THE SUN'S HEAT GIVES THE COMET A TAIL OF GAS AND DUST, FORMING A BRIGHT STREAK IN THE SKY. HALLEY'S COMET IS THE MOST FAMOUS OF THESE "COSMIC SNOWBALLS." IT WAS NAMED FOR THE BRITISH ASTRONOMER EDMOND HALLEY IN 1758. HALLEY REALIZED THAT COMET SIGHTINGS IN 1531, 1607, AND 1682 WERE ACTUALLY ALL SIGHTINGS OF THE SAME COMET. HALLEY'S COMET RETURNS ABOUT EVERY SEVENTY-SIX YEARS. IT WILL BE BACK IN 2061.

Halley's comet, which appears only once every 76 years, streaked across the sky that night. Was the brilliant light a sign? Sam's mother, Jane, hoped so. Her "Little Sammy" had arrived two months early. He was so small and frail that she feared he wouldn't live. In those days, many children—including three of Sam's six brothers and sisters—did not live past childhood. But Sam Clemens survived, and he gave his mother a good deal of trouble in the process.

In 1839, Sam's family moved to the larger town of Hannibal, Missouri. Sam's father, John Clemens, was a lawyer and shopkeeper. John hoped to leave hard times behind.

While John struggled to support the family in Hannibal, Sam struggled to pay attention in school. He attended Mrs. Horr's log schoolhouse on Main Street. Sam was a terrific speller and loved to read, but he was restless and excitable. He often broke the rules or played hooky.

Hannibal was a river town between two bluffs that overlooked the mighty Mississippi River. Sam

called it a "boy's paradise." He and his friends
would sneak away to an island in the river to fish,
swim, and smoke corncob pipes. Other days, they
played in the woods. They pretended to be pirates,
Indians, and Robin Hood and his Merry Men.

There were also caves downriver where the boys went looking for treasure. It was exciting and scary to explore dark, underground passages. Sam once got lost in the caves, and he almost drowned in the river nine times! "You gave me more uneasiness than any child I had," his mother told him. (Sam later said he thought she enjoyed it.)

The Mississippi River brought the world to Sam Clemens's doorstep. In the days before cars or cross-country railroads, the river was one of the country's major highways. More than anything, Sam and his friends wanted to be steamboat men. The great white ships were almost as majestic as the river itself. When Sam heard the call "Steamboat a-comin'!" he and nearly everyone

else in town hurried to the wharf. Sam couldn't take his eyes off the handsome boats or the rough-talking roustabouts who loaded and unloaded their cargo.

Hannibal, Missouri, was a rough place in the 1840s. Missouri had been a state since 1821. Still, it hadn't lost its frontier flavor. When Sam was nine, a shooting took place right outside  his house. Another time he came upon the body of a man who'd been murdered. And he saw a slave killed by a white overseer who simply disliked the way the slave had done a job.

Slavery was a part of Sam Clemens's youth. Hannibal was like most places in the South: White people found ways to excuse the fact that nearly three million blacks were slaves.

STEAMBOAT A-COMIN'!

BEFORE STEAMBOATS, RIVER TRAVEL WAS OFTEN SLOW AND DIFFICULT. BOATS EITHER HAD TO FLOAT DOWNRIVER, WHICH WAS UNPREDICTABLE BECAUSE OF CHANGING CURRENTS, OR THEY HAD TO BE SAILED, TOWED, OR ROWED UPRIVER AGAINST THE CURRENT, WHICH GAVE THEM QUITE A WORKOUT! THOUGH SCIENTISTS KNEW ABOUT THE AWESOME POWER OF STEAM, HARNESSING THAT POWER WAS DANGEROUS. (IF TOO MUCH STEAM IS TRAPPED IN A SMALL SPACE, IT WILL EXPLODE.) IN *1807*, AN INVENTOR NAMED ROBERT FULTON CREATED AMERICA'S FIRST PRACTICAL STEAMBOAT. AFTER THAT, AMERICA HAD A FAST AND DEPENDABLE WAY TO MOVE PEOPLE AND GOODS BOTH *DOWN* AND *UP* THE RIVER.

BY THE LATE *1800s*, TRAINS TOOK OVER MUCH OF THE STEAMBOATS' BUSINESS, BUT STEAMBOATS NEVER LEFT THE RIVERS ENTIRELY. EVEN TODAY, PEOPLE TAKE SIGHTSEEING AND VACATION CRUISES ON THEM.

Slaves belonged to their owners, just like a horse or a dog. "In my schoolboy days," Sam would remember, "I was not aware there was anything wrong about [slavery]." The newspapers said nothing against it; the churches said God approved of it. When Sam's own father had the money, he bought or rented black slaves to help with house- and farm-work.

The slaves Sam knew were also his playmates and friends. Sam spent many weeks each summer at his uncle John Quarles's farm. There, he and his cousins spent evenings in the slave cabins. Sam especially loved listening to a man called Uncle Dan'l, who told folktales and ghost stories by the fire's flickering light.

Sam never forgot the way Uncle Dan'l told a story—the words he used, the rhythm of his speech. His voice would one day inspire Sam's own stories.

Chapter 2
Life on the Mississippi

"Work consists of whatever a body is obliged to do, and play consists of whatever a body is not obliged to do."
—Mark Twain

In March 1847, Sam's father caught pneumonia and died. Sam was only eleven. He felt terrible about his father's death. It wasn't because the two had been close—they hadn't. (Sam said he never saw his father laugh.) But Sam felt bad that he hadn't been a better son.

JOHN CLEMENS
BORN 1798
DIED 1847

The family fell on especially hard times. Jane Clemens had to take Sam out of school and put him to work. He became a printer's apprentice at

the *Missouri Courier* newspaper. In those days, every letter of every word had to be set by hand from individual metal block letters. Sam's job included setting stories in type, running and cleaning the printing press, sweeping the floors, and delivering papers.

In return, Sam received free room and board. He was not paid any money, nor were apprentices

in most trades.
Learning a trade
was considered
payment enough.
Sam's "room" was
a straw mattress

on the floor of the printing office. His "board"
consisted of meals so skimpy that he stole potatoes
and onions from the cellar.

Sam also consumed a steady diet of books—
everything he could get his hands on. In 1850 he

went to work for his older brother, Orion, at the *Hannibal Journal.*

Before long, Sam, now a teenager, began to write. His humorous stories, poetry, and local news were published in the *Journal.* To liven up the paper, he sometimes signed his pieces W. Epaminondas Adrastus Blab, or he caught readers' attention with headlines like:

TERRIBLE ACCIDENT!
500 MEN KILLED AND MISSING!
We had set the above head up expecting (of course)
to use it, but as the accident hasn't happened yet,
we'll say (To be Continued,)

Sam's lively reporting sold more copies of the *Journal,* but Orion didn't appreciate his brother stretching, twisting, and even inventing news. Journalism was supposed to be fact, not fiction. When

Sam was seventeen, he packed his bags. His restless spirit took him first to St. Louis, then to New York, Philadelphia, Keokuk (Iowa), Chicago, and Cincinnati.

Sam worked at various printing jobs in each new place. For a time, he wrote travel letters for the *Keokuk Post*, signing the humorous pieces Thomas Jefferson Snodgrass. Sam had fun writing. To him, it wasn't work. But the printing jobs were boring. Sam later admitted that he did them "lazily, repiningly, complainingly, disgustedly, and always shirking the work when I was not watched."

Sam also wanted to make money—lots of money. So when he read about people making fortunes trading the cocoa plant

COCOA PLAN

in South America, he decided to go there. It was
the first of many get-rich-quick schemes Sam
made the mistake of pursuing. He headed south
on the Mississippi aboard the steamboat *Paul*

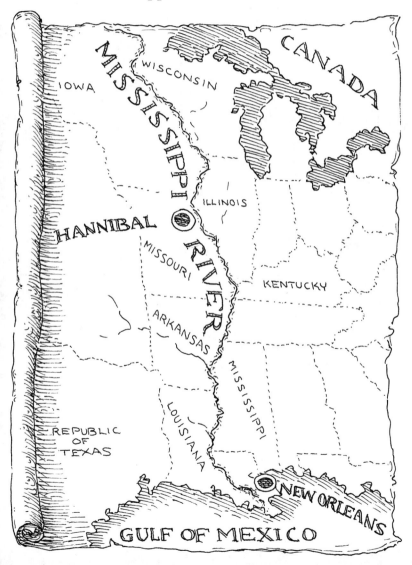

Jones. When he reached New Orleans, however, there were no ships traveling to South America.

Sam went back to the *Paul Jones*. He thought about his childhood dream of being a pilot, and he convinced pilot Horace Bixby to take him on. Sam Clemens was going to become a steamboat man.

"I supposed that all a pilot had to do was to keep his boat in the river, and I did not consider that that could be much of a trick, since it was so wide," Sam later wrote. He soon learned how wrong he was.

A pilot had to memorize every detail of the river—hundreds of miles of river, in fact. He had to know the location of shallows, shipwrecks, and

reefs, where the boat might run aground. He had to be able to read the surface of the water and to keep track of changing currents, shorelines, and water levels. He had to know the river's shape and landmarks so well that he could navigate in rain, darkness, or thick fog.

"I haven't got brains enough to be a pilot," Sam complained to Horace Bixby. "And if I had, I wouldn't have strength enough to carry them around, unless I went on crutches."

Despite what Sam said, he learned quickly. He soaked up everything Bixby told him. He listened for the leadsmen who called out the depth of the water, and he began to read the river like it was a book that always had new stories to tell. One day, Sam would write his own river story, a famous book called *Life on the Mississippi*.

Sam worked on a boat called the *Pennsylvania*. He also found a job for his younger brother, Henry, on the boat.

SAFE WATER?

At certain spots in the river, it was a steamboat leadsman's job to drop a weighted line to the bottom of the water. The line was knotted every six feet, or fathom, to measure the water's depth. A steamboat had to travel in water that was at least twelve feet deep, which was the second mark on the line. When a pilot heard the leadsman call "MARK TWAIN" ("TWAIN" was another word for two), he knew the boat was just barely safe—or just on the edge of danger. It was also a good description of the way Sam Clemens lived his life, so he chose "MARK TWAIN" for his pen name.

HENRY CLEMENS
1838-1858

Then something terrible happened. While Sam was working on another boat—the *Pennsylvania's* boilers blew up. The accident killed about 150 people. Henry was one of them. He was only nineteen years old. For the rest of Sam's life, he blamed himself for Henry's death. But that did not end Sam's steamboat days.

Less than a year later, in April 1859, Sam received his pilot's certificate. Soon he was earning $250 a month—as much, Sam liked to say, as the vice president of the United States. (That wasn't true, but Sam's salary was a good one.) It was

certainly more than his father had ever earned. For the first time in his life, Sam bought expensive clothes and ate fine food.

Sam became master of the boat and master of the crowd. At the wheel or relaxing on deck, Sam

loved to tell stories to the passengers and crew alike.
He also loved the ever-changing sights, voices, and
personalities that were part of life on the river. Sam
was fascinated by people's accents and habits, and by
the river towns' varied flavors and rhythms. He later

said his time on the river was his schooling in human nature and American life.

Chapter 3
Roughing It

"Get your facts first, and then you can distort them as much as you please."

—Mark Twain

Sam might have been a riverboat pilot all his life. But in the spring of 1861, after Abraham Lincoln became president, the Civil War broke out in the United States. Suddenly, Americans were fighting one another. All commercial traffic on the Mississippi River stopped.

ABRAHAM
LINCOLN

The Civil War split the country into the North (the Union) and the South (the Confederacy).

THE CIVIL WAR 1861=1865

FOR DECADES BEFORE THE CIVIL WAR BEGAN, NORTHERN STATES AND SOUTHERN STATES HAD ARGUED OVER SLAVERY. THE NORTH WAS A REGION OF SMALL FARMS AND FACTORIES, WHERE WORKERS WERE PAID FOR THEIR LABOR. THE SOUTH WAS AN AREA WITH MANY LARGE PLANTATIONS THAT DEPENDED ON UNPAID SLAVE LABOR TO BRING IN CROPS LIKE TOBACCO AND COTTON. FOR MANY YEARS, SOUTHERNERS HAD FELT CONTROLLED BY NORTHERN BANKS, WHICH SET THE PRICES FOR THESE CROPS.

IN ALL, ELEVEN SOUTHERN STATES LEFT THE UNION AND FORMED THE CONFEDERATE STATES OF AMERICA. THE NORTH SAID NO STATE HAD THE RIGHT TO DO THAT AND WENT TO WAR IN *1861* TO PRESERVE THE UNION. AFTER THE NORTHERN VICTORY IN *1865*, SLAVERY WAS ABOLISHED. THE FOUR YEARS OF FIGHTING CLAIMED *620,000* LIVES.

Sam did not have strong opinions about the conflict. He made his way home to Hannibal, hoping the war would end quickly. He wanted to return to the river.

Even though it was a slave-holding state where most people sided with the South, Missouri remained part of the Union.

ALABAMA	NORTH CAROLINA
ARKANSAS	SOUTH CAROLINA
FLORIDA	TENNESSEE
GEORGIA	TEXAS
LOUISIANA	VIRGINIA
MISSISSIPPI	

Some of Sam's boyhood pals formed a small unit of Confederate irregulars. (Irregulars were soldiers who were not part of the regular army.) The men called themselves the Marion Rangers. For lack of anything better to do, Sam joined them.

The Marion Rangers spent most of their time hiding from Union troops. "I knew more about retreating than the man that invented retreating," Sam later said. After two weeks, the men were tired and hungry. They called it quits.

Luckily for Sam, his brother Orion had just been named Secretary of the U.S. Territory of Nevada. Pioneers had been settling the West since the Oregon Trail opened in the 1840s. Now Sam would head out there, too, as Orion's personal secretary. Sam didn't feel bad about skedaddling and leaving others to fight the war. He was eager to explore the West.

In July, the brothers climbed aboard a stage-coach for the three-week journey from St. Joseph,

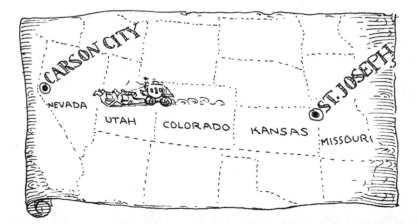

Missouri, to Carson City, Nevada. Sam wrote that they were leaving the States and "all sorts of cares and responsibilities" behind them.

Stagecoaches traveled in stages, stopping every ten to fifteen miles for fresh horses. Their trip was bumpy, crowded, and sometimes dangerous. There were outlaws and hostile Indians, and no

paved roads. But at that time the three-week trip was the fastest way to go west.

For the Clemens brothers, traveling by stagecoach was an adventure. As they made their way across the  Plains, Sam and Orion spied their first buffalo, coyote, jackrabbit, and antelope. They came upon a tribe of Gosiute Indians and had breakfast with an honest-to-goodness outlaw.

Before the coach rolled over the Rocky Mountains and into the desert, Sam gave a "whoop and a hurrah" for a rider of the Pony Express. These young messengers of the legendary mail service barely wasted a moment

when they stopped to change horses. Sam said one horse and rider "came crashing up to the station where stood two men holding fast a fresh, impatient steed, the transfer of rider and mail-bag was made in the twinkling of an eye, and away flew the eager pair and were out of sight before the spectator could get hardly the ghost of a look."

Sam and Orion were almost sorry to arrive in Carson City, their trip had been so exciting. But Carson City had wonders of its own. Instead of trees, it had low, scrubby bushes. Instead of rain, it had fierce dust storms. And instead of wearing a coat, vest, and suspenders, Sam could wear a slouch hat, woolen shirt, and pants stuffed into boot-tops. Yes, Sam liked the West just fine.

In his job as secretary to the Secretary, Sam "had nothing to do and no salary." No matter. There were plenty of ways to get rich in Nevada, where one of the world's largest known silver deposits, the Comstock Lode, had been found in 1859. Carson City was abuzz with "silver fever." Sam confessed, "I succumbed and grew as frenzied as the craziest."

Prospecting for silver was harder than Sam had expected. He and three comrades, weighted down with picks, drills, crowbars, shovels, and cans of blasting powder, "climbed the mountain sides, and

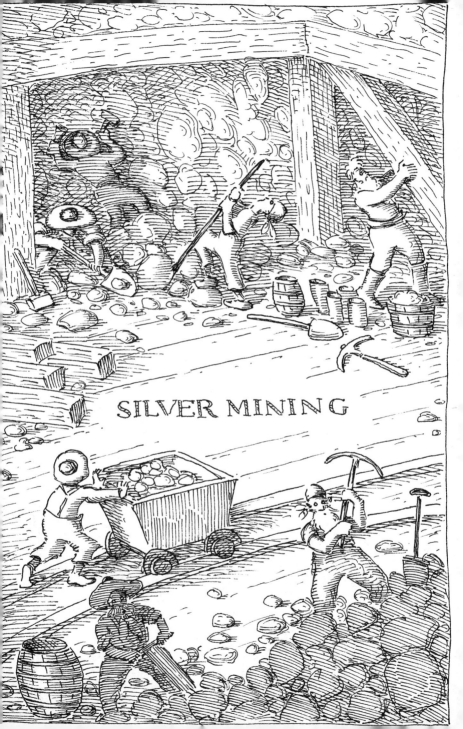

SILVER MINING

clambered among sage-brush, rocks and snow till we were ready to drop with exhaustion, but found no silver. . . . Day after day we toiled, and climbed, and searched."

After six months of digging, shoveling, and drilling into the rocky earth, Sam was still on the "bust" end of the boom-or-bust mining frenzy. He needed a real job.

Sam had written a few sketches and letters about Nevada life for the local newspaper, the *Territorial Enterprise*. The *Enterprise* liked Sam's humorous style. In July 1862, the paper offered him the job of city editor. The position paid twenty-five dollars a week.

Sam hesitated. Did he know how to do the job? Not really. But he needed the money. "I was scared into being a city editor," he would later remember.

As city editor, Sam checked out Virginia City's theaters, saloons, and police stations for leads on exciting stories. When there weren't any, he used

his imagination. For one of his first columns, Sam interviewed a man headed to California in a covered wagon. In his story, he "put this wagon through an Indian fight that to this day has no parallel in history." This was not good journalism, but it was a good story!

Sam's writing was well-suited to the rowdy West. He saw that he had a knack for making stories interesting.

Finally, Sam had found his calling. As he developed his own writing style, he wanted a new name to go with it. Many writers of the day, especially humorists, used pseudonyms, or pen names. But none would become as famous as the one Sam chose on February 3, 1863: Mark Twain.

Chapter 4
The Celebrated Jumping Frog

"The difference between the almost-right word & the right word is really a large matter—it's the difference between the lightning bug and the lightning."
—Mark Twain

After less than a year at the *Enterprise*, Sam wrote to his mother, "Everybody knows me, & I fare like a prince wherever I go."

Sam was growing famous as Mark Twain. His columns were reprinted in California papers and even sometimes in newspapers back East. Soon more people were calling him Mark instead of Sam. (His family and boyhood friends would always call him Sam; others called him Twain or Clemens. The man himself often signed his name "Samuel L. Clemens Mark Twain.")

Mark Twain became known not only for his wit and wisecracks, but also for exposing injustice and fraud. In one column, Mark wrote about an undertaker who was charging sky-high prices for his funerals. The undertaker, Mark said, was taking advantage of families who were too sad to argue about money. Through his pen, Mark tried to correct the evils in society.

Mark wrote freely at the *Enterprise* until a rival newspaperman he'd poked fun at in the news challenged him to a duel—a formal fight with weapons. Rather than risk his life, Mark skipped town for San Francisco.

The beginning of 1865 found Mark Twain prospecting for gold in the hills outside the city. One night around the camp stove, he heard a story that would change his life. It was a tale of a gambler who had made a bet with a stranger. The gambler said his frog could out-jump the stranger's frog. The stranger had no frog; while the gambler went to find a frog for him, the stranger filled the gambler's frog with gunpowder. You'll have to read the story to find out what happens!

Mark wrote down his own version of the simple story, adding comic touches. Then he sent it to an editor in New York City. New York was the nation's literary capital—the big league. "Make your mark in New York," Mark wrote, "and you are a made man."

Before year's end, "Jim Smiley and His Jumping Frog" appeared in the New York *Saturday Press*. One critic said the story was the finest piece of humor ever written in the United States. The "Jumping Frog" was picked up by papers across the country. Within two years, the story became part of Mark Twain's first book, *The Celebrated Jumping Frog of Calaveras County, and Other Sketches*.

Mark's success landed him a plum assignment: traveling to Hawaii for the Sacramento *Union*. At that time, Hawaii was not part of the United States. It was called the Sandwich Islands, and it was ruled by kings and queens. Mark told his

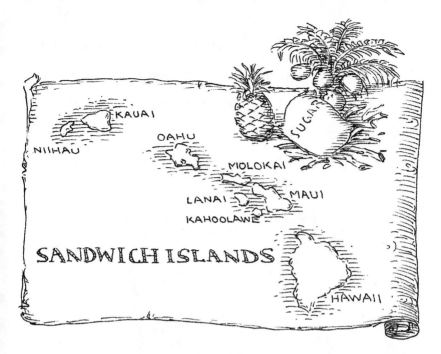

KAUAI

OAHU

NIIHAU

MOLOKAI

LANAI   MAUI

KAHOOLAWE

SANDWICH ISLANDS

HAWAII

readers about the islands' sugarcane plantations, native peoples, and bubbling crater of the volcano Kilauea.

When Mark returned to San Francisco, some friends suggested that his experiences on the trip would be perfect for the lecture circuit. In those days, before radio, television, and movies, people attended lectures to be informed and entertained. A lecturer was a one-man (or one-woman) show.

Mark was terrified, but there was good money and prestige in lecturing, so he decided to give it a try. He rented a hall and printed posters to advertise the event:

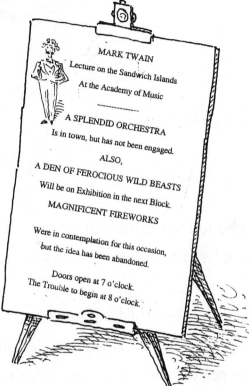

MARK TWAIN
Lecture on the Sandwich Islands
At the Academy of Music

——————

A SPLENDID ORCHESTRA
Is in town, but has not been engaged.
ALSO,
A DEN OF FEROCIOUS WILD BEASTS
Will be on Exhibition in the next Block.
MAGNIFICENT FIREWORKS

Were in contemplation for this occasion,
but the idea has been abandoned.

Doors open at 7 o'clock.
The Trouble to begin at 8 o'clock.

The trouble did begin at eight, when Mark found himself "quaking in every limb with a terror that seemed like to take my life away. The house was full, aisles and all!"

After two minutes on the platform, Mark's stage fright melted. He began speaking in his Southern drawl, pausing at just the right points in his stories to make the crowd laugh. All the while, he acted as if nothing he said was funny.

Mark was a natural in front of an audience. He earned four hundred dollars that night—more than he had in six weeks as a riverboat pilot. Within a month, Mark gave sixteen lectures in California and Nevada, and even one in New York.

Mark was gaining both fame and fortune. But by June 1867, he was restless again. He set sail on the *Quaker City* for a cruise to Europe and the Middle East. Three newspapers sponsored his trip and paid him twenty dollars for each travel letter he sent them.

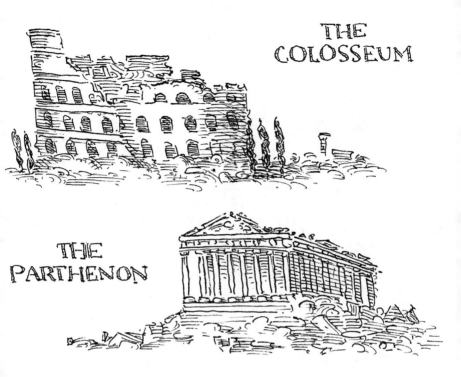

THE COLOSSEUM

THE PARTHENON

Most travelers, and most of Mark's readers, had been taught to respect the treasures of the Old World. The Colosseum in Rome. The Parthenon in Athens. Mark thought people shouldn't accept others' opinions too easily. In his candid and funny letters, he judged for himself whether Europe's artists, palaces, and cities were worthy of their great reputations.

Here is what Mark Twain said about some famous tourist spots:

VENICE

"THE PLACE LOOKED SO LIKE AN OVERFLOWED ARKANSAS TOWN."

MT. VESUVIUS

"I WAS GLAD I VISITED IT, CHIEFLY BECAUSE I SHALL NEVER HAVE TO DO IT AGAIN."

CANCAN DANCERS

"I PLACED MY HANDS BEFORE MY FACE FOR VERY SHAME. BUT I LOOKED THROUGH MY FINGERS."

Mark's letters were so popular in the United States that he returned home a star. A publisher in Hartford, Connecticut, asked him to expand the letters into a book, and he did. *The Innocents Abroad,* published in 1869, was an immediate success.

But the trip to Europe was important for another reason. On board the ship, a fellow traveler named Charles Langdon showed Mark a picture of his sister, Olivia. Mark was charmed by her lovely, delicate face.

Back in New York, Mark was introduced to Olivia, or "Livy." Right away, he knew Livy was the girl for him. She was small and dainty, well-educated, and the most beautiful woman Mark

had ever seen. Her family, unlike Mark's, was wealthy and refined. Their mansion in Elmira, New York, took up an entire block. While Mark grew up skipping prayer meetings (and memorizing Bible verses to make his mother think he'd gone to church), Livy and her family took religion

very seriously. The Langdons even founded a local church after the one they attended refused to stand up against slavery. As abolitionists—people who wanted to end slavery—the Langdons helped runaway slaves escape to freedom.

Mark knew he was "beneath" Livy, but he proposed anyway. She turned him down. Did he give up? No. He promised to become more respectable and give up drinking and swearing. Mark flooded Livy with love letters and proposed three more times.

After three months, Livy said yes. They were married on February 2, 1870.

Chapter 5
The Gilded Age

"My works are like water. The works of the great masters are like wine. But everybody drinks water."
—Mark Twain

"We are two as happy people as you ever saw," Livy wrote soon after the wedding.

The newlyweds moved to Buffalo, New York, where Mark was now part owner—thanks to a

loan from Livy's father—of the *Buffalo Express*. Mr. Langdon's wedding gift was a fully furnished house, plus a cook, maid, and coachman. Mark, or "Youth," as Livy called him, was in heaven. In a letter to the Langdons, Mark described himself as "Little Sammy in Fairyland."

Mark was now also the bestselling author of *The Innocents Abroad*. Mark had worried that critics would pay no attention to his book. But a reviewer from the respected *Atlantic Monthly* praised the book and said Mark Twain was not just a humorist but a writer "quite worthy of the

company of the best." That pleased both Mark and Livy, who was Mark Twain's editor to the end of her days.

Hoping to repeat the success of *The Innocents Abroad*, Mark began *Roughing It*, a book about his time in the West. But it was hard to concentrate on his writing. Livy's father died in August. Then, in November, Livy had her first child, a sickly boy named Langdon. Soon after giving birth, Livy developed typhoid fever. Mark became a frantic, around-the-clock nurse for both his wife and infant son.

Once Livy was better, Mark moved his family to Hartford, Connecticut, for a fresh start. Six months later, a second child, Susy, was born. Susy was healthy and strong. But frail Langdon was still unwell. Ten weeks later, Langdon died of diphtheria.

Mark and Livy were heartbroken. "It seems as if I could not do without [Langdon]," Livy wrote. Throughout his life, Mark Twain believed that "the secret source of humor itself is not joy, but sorrow." And, indeed, his life was marked by much sorrow and tragedy.

But not everything Mark wrote was humorous. In 1873, Mark and his friend Charles Warner wrote a novel called *The Gilded Age*. "Gilded" means covered with a thin

COAL MINING

layer of gold. The book was about a new class of Americans: the super-rich.

Since the Civil War, America's economy was growing more and more powerful. It was no longer based on farming. It was now based on industry: coal mining, oil refining, iron and steel manufacturing, and railroad-building. These big businesses were owned by a few wealthy men who became known as "robber barons." Swindling, lies, bribery, and get-rich-quick schemes were the order of the day. Even government officials were involved. While most workers, many of them newly arrived immigrants, lived in crowded city tenements and barely made a living wage, the robber barons built grand estates and lived like kings. Near the end of the nineteenth century, one robber baron's family threw a party at its seventy-room summer "cottage" in Newport, Rhode Island. The guests dug in a fancy sandbox for diamonds and other gems.

THE BREAKERS, NEWPORT, RHODE ISLAND

THE DARK SIDE OF THE GOLDEN AGE

The Gilded Age wasn't golden for everyone. Millions of Americans lived and worked in dirty, crowded, and even dangerous places. More and more immigrants were coming to America. Many settled in cities on the East Coast where they crowded into tenement apartments in poor neighborhoods. The worst tenements were on the Lower East Side of New York City. Tenements were not well lit or ventilated. In summer, they were dreadfully hot. Several families lived on a floor, squeezed into just one or two rooms. Everyone on a floor shared a single bathroom. And though some people found low-paying jobs in factories, shipyards, or slaughterhouses, others worked long hours right in their rooms, rolling cigars or assembling silk flowers for ladies' hats. These "sweatshop" jobs paid only pennies a day, so everyone in a family, children included, had to work. Such living conditions were a far cry from those of the wealthy. Immigrants endured the hardships with hopes of making a better life for themselves and their children.

The Gilded Age attacked the greed and corruption of business and government. It also criticized Americans' new worship of money, with no concern for how that money was made.

Mark Twain wanted the good life, too; he wanted to give his family what his own father had never been able to. He and Livy built a nineteen-room house with a billiard room, turrets, and porch like a riverboat deck. The home cost $125,000. (The average yearly wage in America at the time was about five hundred dollars.) In addition, there were as many as seven servants and a steady stream of distinguished guests. Mark Twain was rich, but not a robber baron. He felt he earned his money through honest work.

The Hartford home was a happy place for Mark and Livy and their growing family. Just before they moved there, in 1874, a second daughter, Clara, was born. A third daughter, Jean, arrived in 1880. Mark, who was still part child himself, romped on the floor with the girls on his back and dressed up to act in their charades. No wonder Livy called him "Youth"!

The girls loved to climb onto their father's lap and hear his stories. They also listened to the books Mark was writing. Livy would read aloud to the family, her editing pencil in hand. She was a wise and honest critic. Sometimes the girls complained that their mother took out the best parts—but usually those were rude passages their father had purposely put in to make his daughters laugh.

When Susy was thirteen, she wrote a biography of her father. "We are a very happy family," she began. "We consist of Papa, Mamma, Jean, Clara, and me. It is Papa I am writing about, and I shall have no trouble in not knowing what to say about him, as he is a *very* striking character. . . ." Susy went on to describe her father's kind blue eyes and long nose. She continued: "He is a very good man and a very funny one. He *has* got a temper, but we all of us have in this family. . . . He does tell perfectly delightful stories."

Chapter 6
Tom and Huck

"You can't depend on your judgment when your imagination is out of focus."

—Mark Twain

In the summers, Mark, Livy, and the girls went to Quarry Farm, Livy's sister's house in Elmira, New York. After a breakfast of steak and coffee, Mark would disappear to a little hilltop study where he would write and smoke some forty cigars a day. Usually he worked straight through lunch,

his pen streaming across the page. Even after typewriters came into use in the 1870s, Mark Twain preferred to write in longhand.

Mark spent the summers of 1874 and 1875 writing what would become his most popular book: *The Adventures of Tom Sawyer*. Tom Sawyer is based on the young Sam Clemens himself—Tom's about twelve, and full of ideas and mischief. Tom lives in a river town very much like Hannibal in the years before the Civil War. He does what he likes and avoids doing what he doesn't.

In one of the book's most famous scenes, Tom makes the chore of whitewashing a fence look like so much fun that his friends beg him to let them help. Some even pay for the opportunity!

Mark wrote:

Tom resumed his whitewashing and answered carelessly:

"Like it? Well, I don't see why I oughtn't to like it. Does a boy get a chance to whitewash a fence every day?"

That put the thing in a new light. Ben stopped nibbling his apple. Tom swept his brush daintily back and forth—stepped back to note the effect— added a touch here and there—criticised the effect again—Ben watching every move and getting more and more interested, more and more absorbed. Presently he said:

"Say, Tom, let me whitewash a little."

The Adventures of Tom Sawyer was an instant hit with children, but adults read it, too. It is still popular with people of all ages today.

In the summer of 1876, Mark began a sequel to *The Adventures of Tom Sawyer*. This time, Tom's friend Huckleberry Finn was the main character. Huck was ragged and uneducated, but he had a good heart. However, what Mark thought would be another funny boys' adventure story became something much deeper and more serious. Mark put Huck on a raft, floating down the Mississippi with a runaway slave named Jim.

RECONSTRUCTION

THE PERIOD AFTER THE CIVIL WAR WAS KNOWN AS RECONSTRUCTION. THE NATION FACED THE DIFFICULT TASKS OF REBUILDING (RECONSTRUCTING) THE SOUTH, WHERE MOST OF THE FIGHTING HAD TAKEN PLACE, AND REUNITING THE COUNTRY. NEARLY FOUR MILLION FORMER SLAVES WERE BEGINNING LIVES AS FREE PEOPLE, BUT MANY HAD LITTLE OR NO MONEY AND COULDN'T READ OR WRITE.

UNTIL *1877* SOLDIERS FROM THE NORTH WERE STATIONED IN THE SOUTH TO PROTECT BLACKS AND ENSURE THEY WERE ABLE TO VOTE AND HOLD

POLITICAL OFFICE. AFTER NORTHERN SOLDIERS LEFT,
HOWEVER, SOUTHERN WHITES, STILL FURIOUS AT
LOSING THE WAR AND UNABLE TO ACCEPT BLACKS AS
EQUALS, FORMED SECRET SOCIETIES LIKE THE KU KLUX
KLAN. DISGUISED IN WHITE HOODS AND ROBES, KLAN
MEMBERS THREATENED, BEAT, AND SOMETIMES KILLED
BLACKS TO KEEP THEM FROM VOTING AND ASSERTING
THEIR RIGHTS. WHITES SOON REGAINED CONTROL OF
STATE GOVERNMENTS AND PASSED LAWS THAT KEPT
SOUTHERN BLACKS IN ALMOST SLAVE-LIKE CONDITIONS
FOR DECADES.

Jim was very much like the slave Uncle Dan'l; Huck was patterned after Mark's boyhood friend from Hannibal. The characters' friendship raised issues of race, liberty, and right versus wrong. Unsure where to take the story, Mark set it aside.

After a trip to the South, however, Mark was able to work on *The Adventures of Huckleberry Finn* with new energy and confidence. When he finished the manuscript, he said, "*I* shall *like* it, whether anybody else does or not." Mark had written a story that he knew would make many white Americans uncomfortable. He had brought up painful questions of race and racism and faced them directly.

Since meeting Livy and her family, Mark's thoughts about black people in America had changed dramatically. Though he'd had "no aversion" to slavery in his boyhood, he now saw how cruel, how wrong, and how evil it was. What made whites believe that people with darker skin were less human than white people were? Mark put his main character Huck in a pre-Civil War world that was very much like his own as a boy. Huck spends several weeks alone with Jim, the runaway slave. It makes Huck question everything he has been taught by his racist, slave-owning society. In one passage from *Huckleberry Finn*, Huck hears Jim crying and says:

> *[Jim] was thinking about his wife and his children, way up yonder, and he was low and homesick. . . . I do believe he cared just as much for his people as white folks does for their'n. It don't seem natural, but I reckon it's so.*

The Adventures of Huckleberry Finn was an important book for another reason. Mark told the story in Huck's own voice. There is no narrator. The "I" is Huck—he speaks to readers directly. (This is called telling a story in "first person.")

HENRY JAMES

Huck doesn't use correct grammar or fancy words. He just speaks the way an uneducated boy would talk. Writing an entire book in common, American language was something altogether new. Another great American novel called *Washington Square*, written by Henry James, was published in the 1880s. See how different the language is:

Mrs. Penniman was a tall, thin, fair, rather faded woman, with a perfectly amiable disposition, a high standard of gentility, a taste for light literature, and a certain foolish indirectness and obliquity of character. . . . She was not absolutely veracious; but this defect was of no great consequence, for she had never had anything to conceal.

Many critics said *The Adventures of Huckleberry Finn* was trash, and a library in Massachusetts banned the book. *Huckleberry Finn* made some people angry. It made many people think. And it created a distinctly American kind of literature—one that turned everyday American English, with its own rhythms and flavor, into literature.

Mark didn't know it, but he had created one of the greatest American novels of all time.

Chapter 7
Following the Equator

"There are two times in a man's life when he should not speculate: when he can't afford it, and when he can."

—Mark Twain

Mark Twain had started his own company in order to publish *The Adventures of Huckleberry Finn* himself. While Charles L. Webster & Company (named after Mark's nephew and business manager) took orders for the book, Mark went on a four-month lecture tour to earn money.

Webster & Company didn't plan to publish books by other authors. But then Mark learned that former president and Civil War General Ulysses S. Grant was writing his memoirs. Mark offered Grant twice as much money as another publisher had. That clinched the deal. Grant put the finishing touches on his book just days before he died of cancer in 1885. The book was an instant hit. Mark paid Grant's widow nearly $500,000 in profits.

ULYSSES S. GRANT

Grant's bestselling memoirs made Mark rich, too. "It seems to me that whatever I touch turns to gold," Mark marveled. America's most famous author turned fifty that year, and his future had never looked brighter.

The family lived very well. They held elaborate dinners for important guests, including generals William T. Sherman and Philip Sheridan of Civil War fame.

On Friday evenings, Mark's friends gathered in his third-floor study to drink, smoke cigars, and play Mark's favorite game, billiards.

The wild success of Grant's memoirs convinced Mark Twain that book publishing was a better way than writing to make lots of money. He signed Sherman, Sheridan, and others to write books for Charles L. Webster & Company. But none of those books became bestsellers like Grant's.

ALEXANDER GRAHAM BELL

Mark Twain was a brilliant writer, but he was a terrible businessman. It was the age of new inventions; but unfortunately, Mark Twain invested thousands of dollars in all the wrong ones—a steam pulley, a marine telegraph, a mechanical organ, and about one hundred others. Alexander Graham Bell gave Mark Twain the chance to invest in the telephone, but he said no. He didn't think the telephone would catch on with many people.

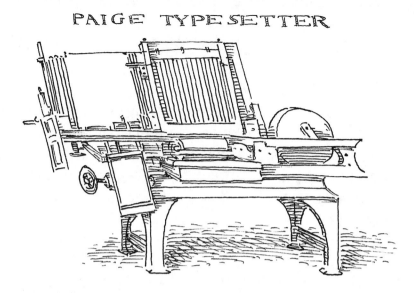

Of all Mark's bad investments, the most disastrous was the Paige typesetter. This enormous machine could set type as fast as several men could by hand, and Mark was convinced that every printing office in the nation—the world, even—would need at least one machine. But the machine had more than eighteen thousand parts, and it kept breaking down. Month after month, for fourteen years, Mark poured his savings and Livy's family money into the typesetter. He was sure it would make his family millions of dollars. It didn't.

THE AGE OF INVENTION

DURING MARK TWAIN'S LIFE, CERTAIN INVENTIONS CHANGED PEOPLE'S LIVES DRAMATICALLY. EVERYDAY CHORES COULD BE DONE FASTER AND MORE EASILY. LIFE BECAME MORE ENJOYABLE, WITH MORE FREE TIME FOR HAVING FUN. MANY OF THESE INNOVATIONS FIRST APPEARED WHEN MARK TWAIN WAS A MIDDLE-AGED MAN.

1873 The first mass-produced typewriters become available

1876 Alexander Graham Bell invents the telephone

1879 Thomas Alva Edison creates an affordable, reliable electric lightbulb

1879 The first skyscraper, Chicago's sixteen-story Leitner Building, opens

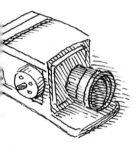

1880 George Eastman patents the first practical roll film for cameras

1883 The Brooklyn Bridge, the longest and highest bridge of its day, is completed and spans New York's East River

1886 The first Coca-Cola is served in Atlanta, Georgia

During this time, Mark wrote *A Connecticut Yankee in King Arthur's Court,* a story of a New Englander who's transported back in time and tries to modernize medieval England. But with bills mounting, the income from Mark's books could not cover the family expenses.

The sad solution was to leave Connecticut and live for a while in Europe, where costs were lower. The family closed up the beloved Hartford home. "We had to leave so much treasured beauty behind," Clara remembered. "We could not look forward with any pleasure to life abroad. We all regarded this break . . . as something resembling a tragedy."

They set sail for France in 1891. Mark kept writing while abroad, but still the debts loomed. In 1894, Webster & Company went bankrupt. Mark owed one hundred thousand dollars. He resolved to pay back every dollar.

During this time, Mark wrote a serious novel titled *Personal Recollections of Joan of Arc*, which he and his family considered his greatest book. But he knew that lecturing was the only way to bring in the kind of money he needed.

So Mark, Livy, and Clara set out on what Mark called "our lecturing raid around the world." (Susy and Jean stayed with their aunt in Elmira.) In just over a year, Mark made nearly one hundred and

fifty appearances. He spoke to sold-out crowds across the United States and in Australia, New Zealand, India, South Africa, and England. Mark was sixty years old and often unwell, and the tour was exhausting. But it made him famous around the world and gave him material for his last travel book, *Following the Equator*.

At last, the tour ended in London in July 1896. Susy, age twenty-four, and Jean, sixteen, were to depart from America and meet Mark, Livy, and Clara in England. It would be a happy family reunion. But Susy never made the journey. She developed spinal meningitis and died August 18.

Mark was devastated. Of the three girls, Susy had been the most like her father. Again, Mark blamed himself for the stress he had caused by bankrupting the family and splitting it apart. On

August 19, he wrote, "I have spent the day . . . reproaching myself for laying the foundation of all our troubles . . . reproaching myself for a million things whereby I have brought misfortune and sorrow to this family."

Chapter 8
Waiting for the Comet

"I was young and foolish then; now I am old and foolisher."

—Mark Twain

"It was a long time before anyone laughed in our household, after the shock of Susy's death," Clara remembered. The family stayed abroad four more years.

When the family returned to America in 1900, Mark received a hero's welcome. He had paid off all his debts with his tour money. The family was back on its feet. Americans had long admired Mark Twain for being a poor, small-town boy who'd become rich and famous. Now they honored and respected him for fighting his way back from financial ruin and upholding his good name. "Always do right," Mark said. "This will gratify some people and astonish the rest."

Rather than return to the Hartford home where Susy had died, the family rented a house in New York City. Guests and reporters called constantly. Mark spoke at luncheons and banquets. He was one of the most famous and recognized people of his day. Mark had something to say about any topic reporters put before him.

NEW YORK CITY CIRCA 1900

Mark Twain, who had always wanted to be more than just a humorist, had become the nation's wise man.

The older Mark Twain grew, the more critical he became. He spoke out against racism, injustice, and the government more than ever. Mark's busy social schedule took a toll on Livy's health. Her heart became so weak that her doctors allowed Mark to spend only a few minutes a day with her. They feared his temperamental nature would

upset her. Mark and Livy wrote notes back and forth, but Mark missed his dearest friend terribly.

In June 1904, Livy died. At her bedside, Mark, Clara, and Jean put their arms around one another and wept as if their hearts would break. Mark had never felt so alone. "She was all our riches, and she is gone," Mark wrote. "She was our breath, she was our life, and now we are nothing." Clara had a nervous breakdown and spent months in the hospital. Jean, who had developed epilepsy, began having terrible seizures and would have to be hospitalized as well. Mark saw his once-happy family torn to pieces.

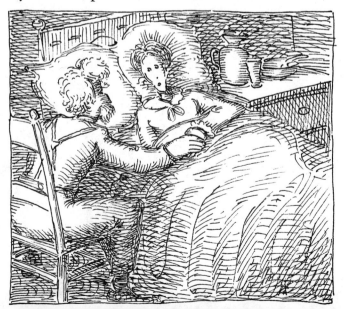

After Livy's funeral, Mark gradually returned to writing short essays. It took him away from his grief. Little by little, he began seeing friends. He was lonely, but he took some comfort in his fame. With his unruly white hair, his bushy mustache and eyebrows, and the white suits he began wearing, Mark Twain was an eye-catching figure. He paraded down Broadway as church let out on Sundays to call attention to himself and bask in strangers' admiration.

Most days, Mark worked on his autobiography, dictating it to a man named Albert Bigelow Paine. And with money from a publisher, Mark built an Italian-style villa near Redding, Connecticut.

Before the villa was ready, Mark traveled to England. There he received an honorary doctorate of letters from Oxford University. Mark's lack of schooling had never bothered him, but he was

thrilled by the great honor and by the crowd's "veritable cyclone of applause."

By the time Mark moved into his new home, he knew he had begun "a holiday whose other end is the cemetery." In 1909, he told a friend, "I came with Halley's comet in 1835. It is coming again next year, and I expect to go out with it."

In October, Clara was married. Jean, still unwell, died of a heart attack that Christmas Eve. Mark wrote down all Jean had meant to him and said, "I shall never write any more."

On April 21, 1910, with Halley's comet blazing into view for the first time since his birth, Mark Twain died.

But he lives on through his wonderful books. Mark Twain once said, "A classic is something that everybody wants to have read and nobody wants to read." But Mark Twain's best books *are* classics, and they *are* read, because they help us understand—and laugh at—ourselves.

SELECTION OF MARK TWAIN'S WORK

The Innocents Abroad (1869)

Roughing It (1872)

The Gilded Age (1873)

The Adventures of Tom Sawyer (1876)

The Prince and the Pauper (1881)

Life on the Mississippi (1883)

The Adventures of Huckleberry Finn (1884)

A Connecticut Yankee in King Arthur's Court (1889)

TIMELINE OF MARK TWAIN'S LIFE

1835 —— Samuel Langhorne Clemens is born November 30 in Florida, Missouri

1839 —— Family moves to Hannibal, Missouri

1847 —— Father dies

1850 —— Works for his brother at the *Hannibal Journal*

1857 —— Becomes a cub pilot on the Mississippi River

1859 —— Receives his steamboat pilot's license

1861 —— Goes west to the Nevada Territory

1863 —— While working for the Virginia City *Territorial Enterprise*, he adopts the pen name Mark Twain

1865 —— "Jim Smiley and his Jumping Frog" is published

1866 —— Goes to Sandwich Islands; Mark gives his first lectures

1867 —— Tours Europe and the Middle East as a travel correspondent

1870 —— Marries Olivia (Livy) Langdon

1874 —— Builds family house in Hartford, Connecticut

1876 —— *The Adventures of Tom Sawyer* is published

1881 —— *The Prince and the Pauper* is published

1884 —— Starts own publishing company and publishes *The Adventures of Huckleberry Finn*

1891 —— Family moves to Europe

1894 —— Publishing company goes bankrupt

1895 —— Mark, Livy, and Clara embark on a worldwide lecture tour

1900 —— Family moves back to the United States

1904 —— Livy dies June 5

1907 —— Receives an honorary doctorate from Oxford University

1910 —— Mark Twain dies April 21

Timeline of the World

Mexican forces lay siege to the Alamo in San Antonio	1836
Samuel Morse invents Morse Code	1838
Charles Goodyear discovers vulcanization of rubber	1839
Potato famine begins in Ireland	1845
Gold is discovered in California	1848
London's Crystal Palace opens for the Great Exhibition	1851
The first modern oil well is drilled near Titusville, Pennsylvania	1858
Charles Darwin publishes *The Origin of Species*	1859
U.S. Civil War begins	1861
President Lincoln's Emancipation Proclamation takes effect	1863
U.S. Civil War ends; President Lincoln is assassinated	1865
First successful transatlantic telegraph cable is laid beneath the ocean	1866
United States buys Alaska from Russia	1867
P. T. Barnum's "Greatest Show on Earth" opens in New York	1871
Harry Houdini is born	1874
General George Armstrong Custer is killed at the Battle of Little Bighorn	1876
Clara Barton founds the American Red Cross	1881
The first U.S. roller coaster opens	1884
Basketball is invented in Massachusetts	1891
Rudyard Kipling publishes *The Jungle Book*	1894
X-rays are discovered	1895
The first modern Olympics are held in Greece	1896
Dr. Sigmund Freud publishes *The Interpretation of Dreams*	1900
The Wright brothers fly the first airplane	1903
The New York City subway opens	1904
Henry Ford sells the first Model T automobile for $850	1908
Boy Scouts of America is incorporated	1910

SELECTED BIBLIOGRAPHY

Clemens, Clara. **My Father Mark Twain**. Harper & Brothers, New York, 1931.

*Cox, Clinton. **Mark Twain: America's Humorist, Dreamer, Prophet**. Scholastic Inc., New York, 1995.

Kaplan, Justin. **Mark Twain and His World**. Simon & Schuster, New York, 1974.

*Lasky, Kathryn. **A Brilliant Streak: The Making of Mark Twain**. Harcourt Brace & Co., San Diego, 1998.

Neider, Charles, ed. **The Autobiography of Mark Twain**. Harper & Brothers, New York, 1959.

*For young readers

Teacher, Lawrence, ed. **The Unabridged Mark Twain, vols. 1–2**. Running Press, Philadelphia, 1997.

Ward, Geoffrey C., Dayton Duncan, and Ken Burns. **Mark Twain: An Illustrated Biography**. Alfred A. Knopf, New York, 2001.